SCHIRMER PERFORMANCE EDITIONS

THE 20TH CENTURY
Elementary Level
33 Pieces by Bartók, Kabalevsky and Shostakovich
in Progressive Order

Compiled and Edited by Richard Walters

T0081336

On the cover:
Marc Chagall
Au Cirque (circa 1911)
DETAIL
Oil on gouache on canvas, (9 1/2 x 13 3/4 in)
© 2015 Artists Rights Society (ARS), New York / ADAGP, Paris
Photo © Christie's Images / Bridgeman Images

ISBN 978-1-4950-1021-7

G. SCHIRMER, *Inc.*

DISTRIBUTED BY
HAL•LEONARD®
CORPORATION
7777 W. BLUEMOUND RD. P.O. BOX 13819 MILWAUKEE, WI 53213

www.musicsalesclassical.com
www.halleonard.com

CONTENTS

Though the table of contents appears in alphabetical order by composer, the music in this book is in progressive order.

COMPOSER BIOGRAPHIES, HISTORICAL NOTES
AND
PRACTICE AND PERFORMANCE TIPS

The pieces in this collection are by some of the greatest composers of the 20th century, composers who wrote a full range of music for orchestra, voices, piano, and chamber ensembles, in the great and large forms. But they also valued music education, and composed interesting music to foster a student pianist's progress. The music by these composers leads a student not only to technical proficiency, but also to become a more fully formed, imaginative musician. Some of these pieces challenge a student to broaden experience beyond conventional, traditional harmony and rhythm. In these works a piano student gets a glimpse into the mind of a great, forward-thinking artistic genius.

In the 20th century composers generally conceived every detail in a composition (unless it is left to chance by design). Many students do not seem to understand the organic role that slurs, phrases, staccatos, accents, dynamics, pedaling, and changes of tempo play in a 20th century composition. Tempo, articulation and dynamics are in mind from the outset of composition, as essential to the music as are the notes and rhythms.

In earlier centuries it was not the custom for the composer to necessarily notate all articulation and pedaling. Insightful understanding of period style of playing informs many of these details in music from the Baroque and Classical eras. Even in music of the 19th century composers did not always notate all such details, and a player's understanding of style is necessary in adding things implied but not stated in the score. Most composers of the 20th century became much more specific about notating such matters. Almost without exception, articulations and dynamics are not editorial suggestions in *The 20th Century* series. They are by the composer and part of the composition. If

editorial suggestions are very occasionally made, they are specifically noted on a piece or indicated in brackets.

Pedaling in *The 20th Century* series is by the composer unless indicated otherwise on an individual piece. Fingering is also often by the composer. Metronome indications without brackets are by the composer. In works where the composer did not provide a suggested metronome indication, those in brackets are editorial suggestions.

The "Practice and Performance Tips" point out a few ideas that may be helpful to the student in learning a piece. These might also be used by a busy teacher as an at-a-glance look at some topics in teaching a piece.

The pieces as part of sets for "children" are actually for progressing pianists of any age. Composers needed a way to indicate to the world that the pieces were written for a contained level of difficulty and for students, and were to be thought of differently from concert works such as a sonata or concerto, for example. The tradition of titling these with some variation along the lines of a "children's album" was a convenient way of solving this. It has always been understood, and certainly by the composers themselves, that this music is about the level of the pianist, not the age of the pianist.

When a great talent turns attention to writing a short piece of limited difficulty level for students, it is approached with the same aesthetics, temperament, tastes and creative invention applied when composing a symphony, opera or concerto. These exquisite miniatures are complete works of timeless art. Through them a master musician of the past indirectly teaches a progressing musician of the present and the future.

BÉLA BARTÓK
(1881–1945, Hungarian; became a US citizen in 1945)

Béla Bartók is one of the most important and often performed composers of the twentieth century, and much of his music, including *Concerto for Orchestra*, his concertos, his string quartets, and his opera *Bluebeard's Castle*, holds a venerable position in the classical repertoire. His parents were amateur musicians who nurtured their young son with exposure to dance music, drumming, and piano lessons. In 1899 he started piano and composition studies at the Academy of Music in Budapest and not long after graduation he joined the Academy's piano faculty. Bartók wished to create music that was truly Hungarian at its core, a desire that sparked his deep interest in folk music. His work collecting and studying folksongs from around the Baltic region impacted his own compositional style greatly in terms of rhythm, mood, and texture. Bartók utilized folk influences to create a truly unique style. Though he composed opera, concertos, ballets, and chamber music, he was also committed to music education and composed several piano works for students, including his method *Mikrokosmos*. Bartók toured extensively in the 1920s and '30s, and became as well-known as both a pianist and composer. He immigrated to the US in 1940 to escape war and political turmoil in Europe, and settled in New York City, though the last years of his life were difficult, with many health problems.

Selections from *The First Term at the Piano,* Sz. 53, BB 66 (composed 1913)

With the original Hungarian title *Kezdők zongoramuzsikája*, these 18 short pieces were selected from the 44 pieces Bartók composed for a piano method by Bartók and Sándor Reschofsky, published in 1913. The pieces were composed for piano students at Reschofsky's music school in Budapest. Some of the pieces are based on folksongs, others are original compositions. Fingerings, articulation and metronomic markings are by Bartók. After a series of setbacks and disappointments Bartók composed little in the years 1912–1914. His international acclaim and successful concert tours lay ahead, in the 1920s. The little pieces in *The First Term at the Piano* were the great composer's only compositions in 1913. In the previous year, 1912, Bartók prepared teaching editions of Bach, Beethoven, Haydn and Mozart which became standard pedagogical publications in Hungary.

Stepping Stones
Practice and Performance Tips
- As a companion exercise, practice a smooth five-finger pattern in both hands, from C to G and back down.
- This simple piece asks for an elegant phrase over three measures, played at *f*.
- Smoothly move from note to note.

- There may be a slight crescendo and then decrescendo in each phrase.
- Use no pedal at all.

Invention I
Practice and Performance Tips
- Though the composer has asked for *f*, the piece needs legato and elegant phrasing.
- Practice hands separately in making a graceful phrase; then hands together, first slowly.
- Pay special attention to the composer's phrase markings.
- Your practice should lead to a steady, flowing line.
- Use no pedal at all.

Parallel Lines
Practice and Performance Tips
- The hands play in octaves throughout
- The composer asks for graceful two-measure phrases.
- The hands begin in a five-finger position with the third finger on B.
- Both hands change to a different five-finger position in measure 9, with the third finger on F-sharp.
- Both hands return to the third finger on B in measure 17, and remain in that position until the end.
- The composer has not indicated a dynamic for this teaching piece, almost certainly deliberately.
- Practice this piece with a variety of dynamics, from soft to loud.
- Always make a graceful phrase a priority, no matter what the volume.
- One can imagine a tempo faster than Bartók's suggested metronome marking.
- Use no pedal at all.

Legato and Staccato
Practice and Performance Tips
- In the first line the hands play with the same articulation.
- Practice hands separately at first, playing legato or staccato as marked.
- Exactly execute the articulation that Bartók has composed, noting the phrasing and staccato markings.
- In the second line of music the hands must independently play different articulation.
- Though *f*, play with a graceful touch.
- Bartók's metronome indication is quite slow, and may be too slow for some.
- Use no pedal at all.

Dialogue I
Practice and Performance Tips
- Practice hands separately before practicing hands together.
- Play the phrasing as indicated.
- Each hand has its own, independent phrasing.
- Initial practice can be at *mf*.
- After mastering the piece, move to a gentle legato touch and play *p*.

- This little piece is an introduction to counterpoint, with two independent voices combined.
- Use no pedal at all.

Dialogue II
Practice and Performance Tips
- Practice hands separately before practicing hands together.
- Play the phrasing gracefully, as indicated.
- Each hand has its own, independent phrasing.
- The composer (almost certainly deliberately) did not indicate a dynamic for this teaching piece.
- Initial practice can be at *mf*.
- After mastering the piece, play at different dynamics, from *p* to *f*.
- Use no pedal at all.

Dialogue III
Practice and Performance Tips
- Practice hands separately before practicing hands together.
- Play the phrasing gracefully, as indicated.
- Each hand has its own, independent phrasing.
- Though primarily written in *legato* phrases, the composer has indicated that some notes should be accented.
- Initial practice can be at *mf*, and at a slow and steady tempo.
- After mastering the piece, move to playing *f* as indicated, but retain a smooth, *legato* touch.
- Use no pedal at all.

Follow the Leader
Practice and Performance Tips
- The piece is constructed in three four-measure phrases.
- The left hand leads in measures 1, 3 and 5, but in measures 2, 4 and 6–8 becomes accompaniment.
- Bartók's brief composition has vivid and essential details of accents, articulation and phrasing.
- Make certain to exactly execute all dynamics and articulations.
- The *sforzando* (*sf*) is to be played stronger than the accent (>).
- Keep the rhythm just as crisp in the middle soft section as in the surrounding loud sections.
- Measure 6 to the end requires independence of the hands in phrasing and articulation.
- Though Bartók's tempo is slow, your initial practice tempo can be even slower.
- Use no pedal at all.

Short and Long Legato
Practice and Performance Tips
- Each hand is in a five-finger position, A to E.
- The "short legato" of the title refers to the one bar phrases, such as right hand measures 1–4.
- The "long legato" of the title refers to the long

phrase in the left hand measures 1–4, or both hands measures 9–14.
- Notice how the few staccato notes create pleasing contrast in the musical texture.
- The entire piece needs a quiet, gentle touch.
- In measures 1–4 and 10–14 slightly bring out the melody in the right hand, with the left hand an accompaniment.
- Bartók's metronome indication is quite slow. Some may want to take the piece a bit faster.
- Create legato entirely with the fingers. Use no pedal at all.

Peasant Song from *Ten Easy Pieces,* Sz. 39, BB 51 (composed 1908)

Bartók collected and documented thousands of folksongs from Hungary and neighboring countries. This folk music influenced his own compositions throughout his subsequent career, but especially in the initial years of its impact, 1904–1910. Bartók made "art music" settings of folksongs, and also created compositions that are in the spirit of folk music. It is often not clear which of these is at work in a piece by Bartók, because the composer didn't necessarily document which pieces were based on folksongs and which are original compositions in that style. This approach applies to *Ten Easy Pieces*.

Practice and Performance Tips
- Though the hands play the same notes in octaves throughout, the piece is not simple.
- Though it begins *f*, because Bartók subsequently states *più f*, restrain the volume at the beginning.
- Phrasing is very important to give this haunting melody shape and weight.
- Carefully notice the many details of articulation and dynamics, including notes with accents and tenuto markings.
- The "swells" (rise and fall in volume) will give the phrases shape.
- Legato should be accomplished with the fingers only. Use no pedal at all.

DMITRI KABALEVSKY
(1904–1987, Russian)

Kabalevsky was an important Russian composer of the Soviet era who wrote music in many genres, including four symphonies, a handful of operas, theatre and film scores, patriotic music, choral music, vocal music, and numerous piano works. He embraced the Soviet notion of socialist realism in art, a fact that was more than politically advantageous to his career in the USSR. While studying piano and composition at the Moscow Conservatory, he taught piano lessons at a music college and it was for these students that he began writing works for young players. In 1932 he began teaching at the Moscow Conservatory, earning the title of professor in 1939. He eventually went on to develop programs for the concert hall, radio, and television aimed at teaching children about classical music. In the last decades of his life, Kabalevsky focused on developing music curricula for schools, retiring from the Moscow Conservatory to teach in public schools where he could test his theories and the effectiveness of his syllabi. This he considered his true life's work, and his pedagogical principles revolutionized music education in Russia. A collection of his writings on music education was published in English in 1988 as *Music and Education: A Composer Writes About Musical Education.*

Selections from *24 Pieces for Children*, Op. 39 (composed 1944)

Kabalevsky began writing piano music for students as early as 1927. His first major set, *30 Children's Pieces* of Op. 27, was composed in 1937–38. The *24 Pieces for Children* (alternately titled *24 Easy Pieces*) of Op. 39 is for an earlier level of study than Op. 27. Though Kabalevsky composed operas, orchestral music, concertos and chamber music throughout his career, as well as more difficult piano literature, he returned to writing music for piano students periodically in his life, reflecting his deeply felt commitment to music education.

Melody, Op. 39, No. 1
Practice and Performance Tips
- Make a graceful phrase in both hands.
- Practice hands separately in making the phrase.
- If small hands cannot use the fingers only in the left hand to play legato, very sparing use of the sustaining pedal can be used to create the smooth movement from chord to chord.
- Note the dynamic contrasts, with a sudden *p* in measure 5, followed by a crescendo.

Polka, Op. 39, No. 2
Practice and Performance Tips
- For the first time in the progressive order of the book the melody moves to the left hand.
- The right hand plays an accompaniment.
- Practice hands separately.
- Note the smooth phrasing in the left hand and the staccato markings in the right hand.
- Then slowly practice hands together, exactly retaining the articulation Kabalevsky has composed.
- The challenge is to combine playing the left hand smoothly and the right hand staccato.

Rambling, Op. 39, No. 3
Practice and Performance Tips
- Note the combination of staccato and sustained notes (with tenuto markings) in the right hand.
- Practice right hand only, carefully playing the composed articulations.
- Play the staccato/tenuto combination in the left hand as if it were an eighth note followed by an eighth rest.
- Practice hands together slowly, executing all the articulation exactly as composed.
- Use no pedal at all.

Cradle Song, Op. 39, No. 4
Practice and Performance Tips
- Both hands play the same notes, in octaves, throughout. First practice hands separately.
- Practice may begin at *mf*.
- After becoming secure in the piece, then play softly and gently, but steadily.
- Create the two-note slur with legato, with a very slight lift before the next two-note slur.
- Note the composer's tempo marking of *poco lento*.
- Think of the tempo as gently rocking a baby's cradle back and forth.
- Use no pedal at all.
- Possible slight *ritard.* in the final bar leading to the final note.

Playing, Op. 39, No. 5
Practice and Performance Tips
- All notes are staccato throughout, except the final note of the piece.
- The composer skillfully passes the musical line from right hand to left hand and back.
- Each staccato note should be played evenly, with the same volume and crisp shortness.
- Practice hands together, first at a slow but steady practice tempo.
- As you master the music, slowly increase your practice tempo, but always maintain a steady beat.
- You should have fun playing this piece. Note the title!
- Use no pedal at all.

Funny Event, Op. 39, No. 7
Practice and Performance Tips
- The entire piece is constructed of two-measure phrases, with one hand imitating the other.
- Every note is played staccato.
- Note the accents on the downbeats of measures 1–8 and measures 17–24.
- There are three sections to the form: measures 1–8, measures 9–16, and measures 17–24 (repeat of measures 1–8).
- Though still staccato, the dynamics and texture are markedly different in the middle section.
- Your practice tempo can begin as slow as necessary to keep a steady beat.
- Gradually increase the tempo in your practice as you master the music, maintaining steadiness whatever the tempo.
- Your performance should be playful and witty, to reflect the title.
- Use no pedal at all.

Song, Op. 39, No. 8
Practice and Performance Tips
- Each measure of the piece is a graceful phrase.
- Make sure the right hand and left hand are equal in volume.
- Make sure both hands are perfectly united in phrasing.
- A piece with "Song" in the title needs to having a singing, smooth tone.
- Create legato and phrasing entirely with the fingers
- Use no pedal at all.

A Little Dance, Op. 39, No. 9
Practice and Performance Tips
- The entire piece is played staccato except the last chord.
- The piece is constructed in three four-measure phrases.
- Practice each hand separately, first slowly, playing with an even, staccato touch.
- Make sure the left-hand staccato chords are crisply played.
- Emphasize the contrast between *f* and *p*.
- After hands alone, move to hands together practice at a slow tempo, continuing to play staccato.
- As you master the piece, increase the tempo until you can play *Allegro molto* at a steady pace.
- Use no pedal at all.

Scherzo, Op. 39, No. 12
Practice and Performance Tips
- This short piece can create a brilliant effect.
- Because it is so short when played at a fast tempo, one might repeat the entire piece.
- Practice should begin hands together at a slow tempo.
- From the beginning of practice, learn the articulation with the notes.
- Note the slurred three notes in the left hand, answered by two notes marked staccato in the right hand.
- The contrast between the slur and the staccato creates the essential character of the music.
- Use no pedal at all.

Selections from 35 *Easy Pieces*, Op. 89
(composed 1972–74)
Kabalevsky's last large set of piano pieces for students was composed in his late sixties, after a lifetime of experiences with young musicians, and after he had long since attained a revered position as the cultural leader of music education in the USSR. These were also his last compositions for piano. After 1974 Kabalevsky only wrote a few more compositions, which were songs or small choral pieces.

First Piece, Op. 89, No. 1
Practice and Performance Tips
- Make a graceful phrase in the right hand, and answer it with a graceful phrase in the left hand.
- Smoothly pass the phrase from the right to the left hand in measures 9–10 and 11–12.
- Note the progression from *p* to *mf* and back to *p* in this brief piece.
- Gently and gracefully cross the left hand over for the final note.
- Use no pedal at all.

First Etude, Op. 89, No. 2
Practice and Performance Tips
- Though relatively simple, this etude is musically challenging.
- The composer asks the player to create a four-measure phrase moving from hand to hand.
- The music also puts the hands close together in spots, creating additional challenges.
- Though marked *mf*, Kabalevsky has also indicated *Tranquillo*; the music needs a gentle flow.
- Do not take this etude too quickly.
- Create the legato and phrase completely with the fingers. Use no pedal at all.

Quiet Song, Op. 89, No. 3
Practice and Performance Tips
- The right hand changes position in measure 4, then again in measures 7, 11 and 14.
- The left hand changes position in measures 6 and 13.
- Take special note of the composer's phrase markings, and smoothly pass the phrase from the right to the left hand.
- Practice at *mf* until you are confident, then begin practicing at *p*. Note the title of the piece!
- *Cantabile* means a singing tone, which implies smooth playing.
- Use no pedal at all.

At Recess, Op. 89, No. 4
Practice and Performance Tips
- The piece is comprised of three elements: two-note slurs, staccato notes, and four-note phrases.
- Each element must be precisely played to create the playful spirit of "At Recess."
- Make certain to smoothly move from right hand to left hand in measures 8 and 15.
- Though played *f*, this piece still requires a buoyant touch.
- Practice slowly with both hands together.
- Use no pedal at all.

First Waltz, Op. 89, No. 5
Practice and Performance Tips
- The melody is in the left hand throughout.
- Note that Kalalevsky has added tenuto stress marks to the melody.
- The right hand is accompaniment, and should be played slightly softer than the left hand.
- Practice each hand separately at first.
- Be sure to play a legato phrase in the left hand as

marked, measures 5–8 and 9–12.

- Kabalevsky's tempo of *Non allegro* warns you not to play this rather sad piece too quickly.
- Use no pedal at all.

Light and Shadow, Op. 89, No. 7
Practice and Performance Tips
- The "light" is the loud music; the "shadow" is the soft music.
- Notice the contrast between the staccato markings and those notes without staccato.
- Be careful not to play all notes staccato.
- First practice hands separately, slowly.
- Then practice hands together, slowly.
- Retain the composed articulation in your practice, no matter what tempo.
- Use no pedal at all.

Little Hedgehog, Op. 89, No. 8
Practice and Performance Tips
- Notice that every note of the piece is played staccato, with the final three notes also accented.
- Kabalevsky has indicated *staccatissimo*, meaning extremely short, crisp staccato.
- Practice right and left hands separately, and initially at a slow tempo.
- The sudden *p* in measure 8 followed by the crescendo creates a fun effect.
- Use no pedal at all.

Playful One, Op. 89, No. 10
Practice and Performance Tips
- Gracefully cross the left hand over the right hand in measures 4, 6, 10 and 12.
- Practice hands together, first at a slow tempo.
- Notice the two- and three-note slurs that Kabalevsky has composed.
- Accurately playing the slurs as composed will make the piece "playful."
- Use no pedal at all.

Trumpet and Echo, Op. 89, No. 15
Practice and Performance Tips
- The right hand is the trumpet and the left hand is the echo.
- The right hand plays *f*, with each note articulated and accented.
- In contrast, the left hand plays softly and legato, moving from note to note smoothly.
- The composer's marking *marcato* refers to the right hand only.
- Practice hands together, first at a slow tempo.
- Use no pedal at all.

Evening Song, Op. 89, No. 16
Practice and Performance Tips
- Practice first hands together slowly.

- Note that the composer passes the legato phrase from the right hand to the left hand.
- When the dynamic moves to *mf*, the texture changes to short two-note phrases in the right hand.
- Note the stressed notes in measures 13–14, which will help make the two-note phrases.
- A slight *ritard.* in the final measure is possible, leading to the final note.
- *Andante cantabile* indicates careful attention to the smooth, flowing phrase throughout.
- Use no pedal at all.

Skipping Rope, Op. 89, No. 17
Practice and Performance Tips
- Practice hands together, first at a slow tempo.
- Play staccato throughout, except for the last accented note.
- Practice hands together, first at a slow tempo.
- The trickiest challenge in this piece is hands crossing each other.
- Right hand crosses left hand in measures 3 and 7.
- Left hand crosses right hand in measures 10 and 12.
- The words *accel. poco a poco al fine* mean to accelerate the tempo little by little until the end.
- Use no pedal at all.

Trumpet and Drum, Op. 89, No. 20
Practice and Performance Tips
- The left hand represents the drum throughout, which should be played *marcato* and very steadily.
- The right hand is the trumpet.
- Accurately play the two-note slurs in the right hand.
- Carefully and enthusiastically play the accents as the composers has indicated.
- Even though the piece begins *f*, in measure 13 the composer asks for even more volume.
- Use no pedal at all.

DMITRI SHOSTAKOVICH
(1906–1975, Russian)

A major mid-20th century composer, Shostakovich is famous for his epic symphonies, concertos, operas, string quartets, and other chamber works. Born in St. Petersburg, his entire career took place in Soviet-era Russia. His life teetered between receiving high official honors and living with an almost debilitating fear of arrest for works that did not adhere to the Soviet ideals of socialist realism. In 1934, his opera *Lady Macbeth of the Mtsensk District* met with great popular success, but was banned by Stalin for the next thirty years as modernist, surrealist, and obscene. The following year, Stalin began a campaign known as the Purges, executing or exiling to prison camps politicians, intellectuals and artists. Shostakovich managed to avoid such a fate, and despite an atmosphere of anxiety and repression was able to compose an astounding number of works with originality, humor, and emotional power. He succeeded in striking a balance between modernism and tradition that continues to make his music accessible to a broad audience. An excellent pianist, Shostakovich performed concertos by Mozart, Prokofiev, and Tchaikovsky early in his career, but after 1930 limited himself to performing his own works and some chamber music. He taught instrumentation and composition at the Leningrad Conservatory from 1937–1968, with brief breaks due to war and other political disruptions, and at the Moscow Conservatory in the 1940s. Since his death in 1975, Shostakovich has become one of the most performed 20th century composers.

Selections from *Children's Notebook for Piano*, Op. 69 (composed 1944–45)

Among a huge output of symphonies, operas and chamber music, Shostakovich wrote only a few pieces for piano students. *Children's Notebook for Piano* was written for his eight-year-old daughter, Galina, for her studies on the instrument. The original set was published as six pieces. The seventh piece, "Birthday," written for Galina's ninth birthday in 1945, was added in a later edition.

March, Op. 69, No. 1

Practice and Performance Tips

- Every note is marked with a composed slur, staccato, accent or tenuto.

- Learn the articulations along with the notes from the very beginning, so that they are organically part of the music.
- Make the most of the wide range of dynamic contrasts, from *p* to *f*.
- A march requires a particularly steady beat. Begin with a slow practice tempo.
- Use no pedal at all.

Waltz, Op. 69, No. 2

Practice and Performance Tips

- The melody is in the right hand throughout; the left hand is accompaniment.
- Play the right-hand melody with slightly more volume than the left hand.
- Shostakovich has deliberately indicated *non legato*. Play *portato*, which is a slight separation between notes.
- Notice the *dim.* and *rit.* in measures 15 and 16, before returning to the tempo in measure 17.
- The piece could be very well played with no pedal throughout, or careful touches of pedal could be added.

— Richard Walters, editor
*Joshua Parman, Charmaine Siagian
and Rachel Kelly, assistant editors*

12

First Piece
from *35 Easy Pieces*

Dmitri Kabalevsky
Op. 89, No. 1

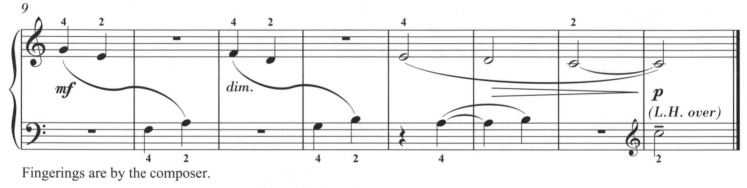

Fingerings are by the composer.

Stepping Stones
from *The First Term at the Piano*

Béla Bartók

Fingerings are by the composer.

Melody
from *24 Pieces for Children*

Dmitri Kabalevsky
Op. 39, No. 1

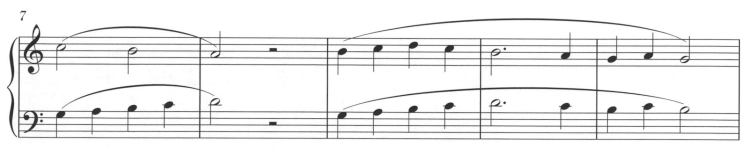

Fingerings are editorial suggestions.

Invention I
from *The First Term at the Piano*

Béla Bartók

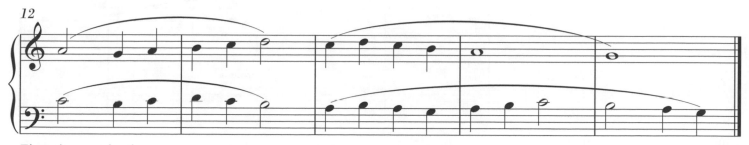

Fingerings are by the composer.

Cradle Song
from *24 Pieces for Children*

Dmitri Kabalevsky
Op. 39, No. 4

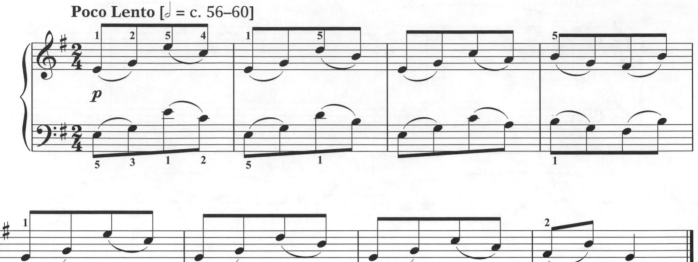

Fingerings are editorial suggestions.

Quiet Song
from *35 Easy Pieces*

Dmitri Kabalevsky
Op. 89, No. 3

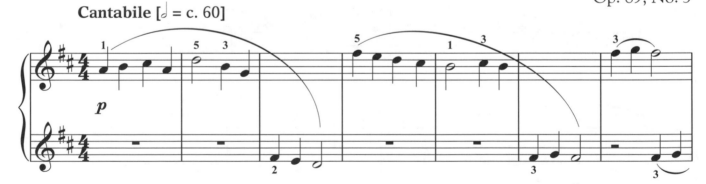

Fingerings are by the composer.

Rambling
from *24 Pieces for Children*

Dmitri Kabalevsky
Op. 39, No. 3

Fingerings are editorial suggestions.

Polka
from *24 Pieces for Children*

Dmitri Kabalevsky
Op. 39, No. 2

Fingerings are editorial suggestions.

16

Light and Shadow
from *35 Easy Pieces*

Dmitri Kabalevsky
Op. 89, No. 7

Fingerings are by the composer.

Parallel Lines
from *The First Term at the Piano*

Béla Bartók

Fingerings are by the composer.

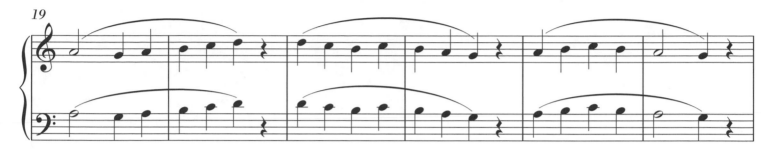

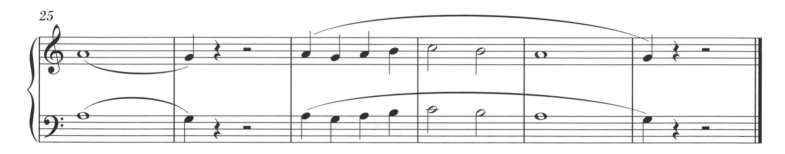

Evening Song
from *35 Easy Pieces*

Dmitri Kabalevsky
Op. 89, No. 16

Andante cantabile [♩ = c. 66]

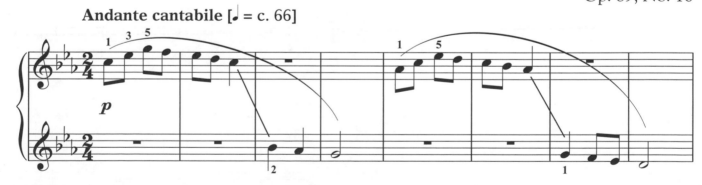

Fingerings are by the composer.

18

Trumpet and Echo
from *35 Easy Pieces*

Dmitri Kabalevsky
Op. 89, No. 15

Fingerings are by the composer.

Playing
from *24 Pieces for Children*

Dmitri Kabalevsky
Op. 39, No. 5

Fingerings are editorial suggestions.

Legato and Staccato
from *The First Term at the Piano*

Béla Bartók

Fingerings are by the composer.

Dialogue I
from *The First Term at the Piano*

Béla Bartók

Fingerings are by the composer.

20

Dialogue II
from *The First Term at the Piano*

Béla Bartók

Fingerings are by the composer.

Dialogue III
from *The First Term at the Piano*

Béla Bartók

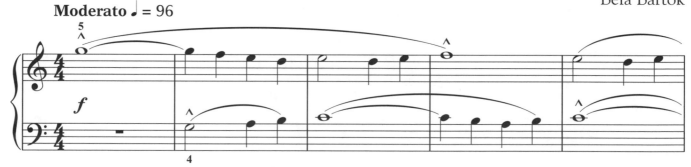

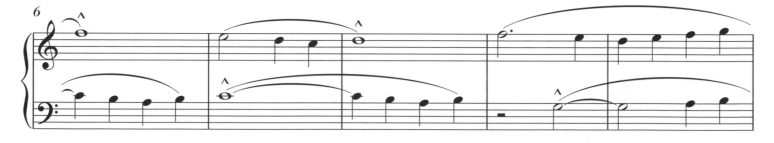

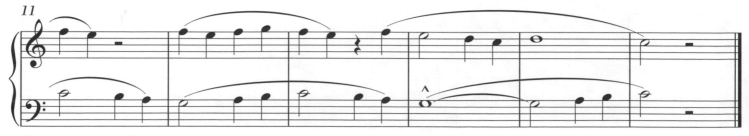

Fingerings are by the composer.

Follow the Leader
from *The First Term at the Piano*

Béla Bartók

[Adagietto] ♩ = 66

Fingerings are by the composer.

Short and Long Legato
from *The First Term at the Piano*

Béla Bartók

Moderato ♩ = 52

Fingerings are by the composer.

A Little Dance
from *24 Pieces for Children*

Dmitri Kabalevsky
Op. 39, No. 9

Allegro molto [♩ = c. 96]

Fingerings are editorial suggestions.

Song
from *24 Pieces for Children*

Dmitri Kabalevsky
Op. 39, No. 8

Andante [♩ = c. 72]

Fingerings are editorial suggestions.

Funny Event
from *24 Pieces for Children*

Dmitri Kabalevsky
Op. 39, No. 7

Fingerings are editorial suggestions.

At Recess
from 35 Easy Pieces

Dmitri Kabalevsky
Op. 89, No. 4

Allegro [♩ = c. 120]

Fingerings are by the composer.

Little Hedgehog
from 35 Easy Pieces

Dmitri Kabalevsky
Op. 89, No. 8

Allegretto staccatissimo [♩ = c. 104]

Fingerings are by the composer.

Skipping Rope
from *35 Easy Pieces*

Dmitri Kabalevsky
Op. 89, No. 17

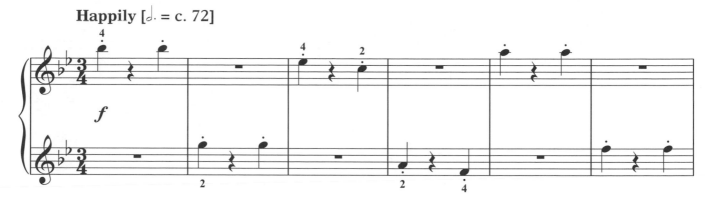

Fingerings are by the composer.

Playful One
from *35 Easy Pieces*

Dmitri Kabalevsky
Op. 89, No. 10

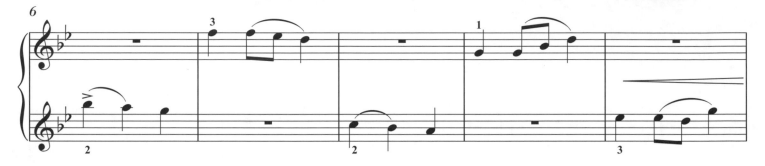

Fingerings are by the composer.

First Waltz
from *35 Easy Pieces*

Dmitri Kabalevsky
Op. 89, No. 5

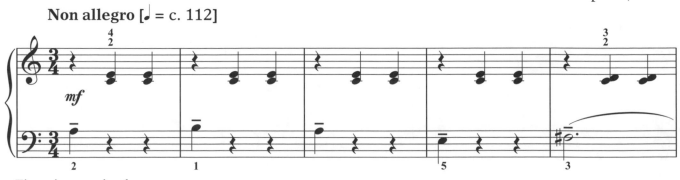

Fingerings are by the composer.

First Etude
from *35 Easy Pieces*

Dmitri Kabalevsky
Op. 89, No. 2

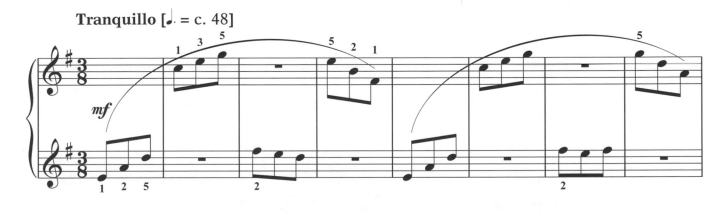

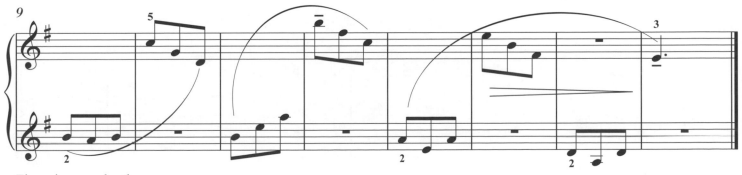

Fingerings are by the composer.

Peasant Song
from *Ten Easy Pieces*

Béla Bartók

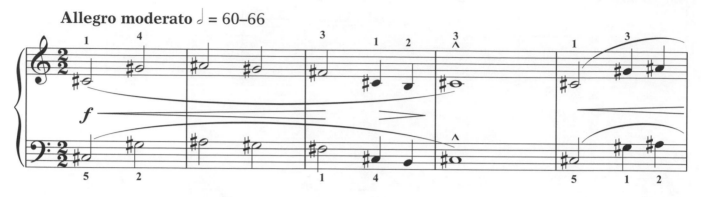

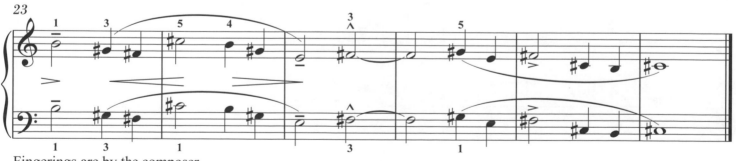

Fingerings are by the composer.

Waltz
from *Children's Notebook for Piano*

Dmitri Shostakovich
Op. 69, No. 2

Alla valzer [♩. = c. 60]

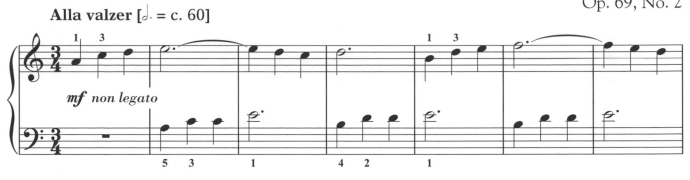

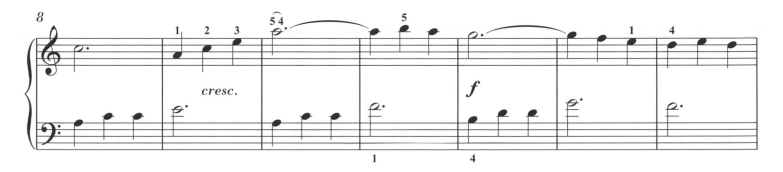

Fingerings are editorial suggestions.

March
from *Children's Notebook for Piano*

Dmitri Shostakovich
Op. 69, No. 1

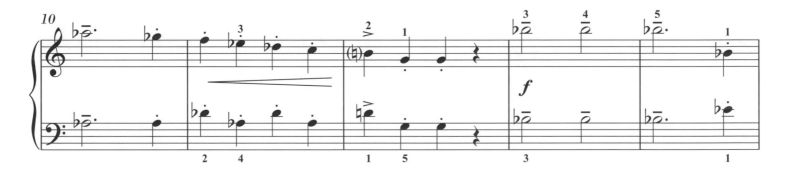

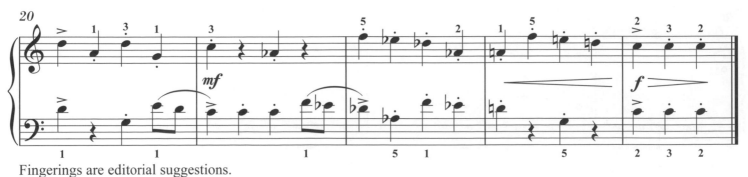

Fingerings are editorial suggestions.

Trumpet and Drum
from *35 Easy Pieces*

Dmitri Kabalevsky
Op. 89, No. 20

Marziale [♩ = c. 72]

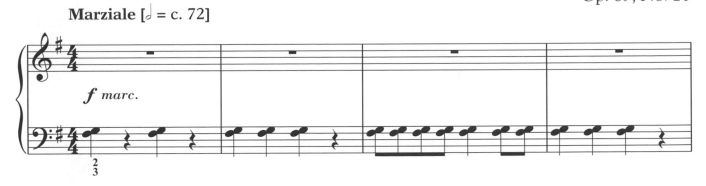

Fingerings are by the composer.

Scherzo
from *24 Pieces for Children*

Dmitri Kabalevsky
Op. 39, No. 12

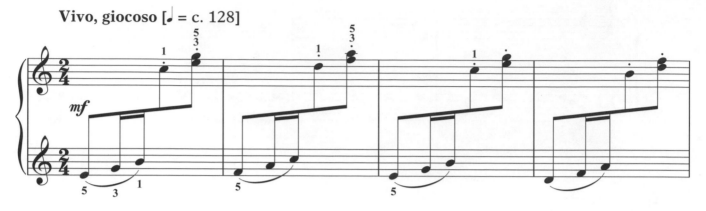

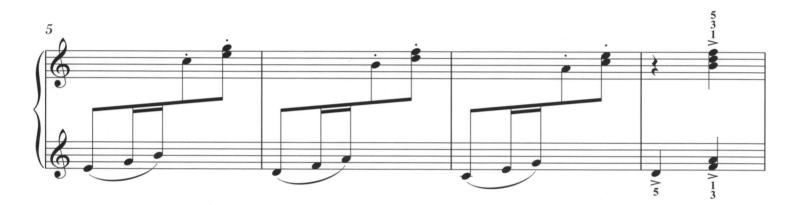

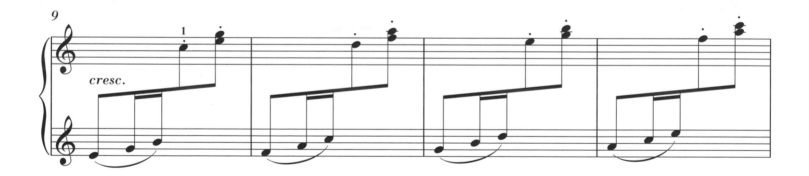

Fingerings are editorial suggestions.